From Grief to Celebration:

How One Family Learned to Embrace the Gift of Down Syndrome

From Grief to Celebration:

How One Family Learned to Embrace the Gift of Down Syndrome

By:
Margaret (Gary) Bender

Cover design:
Alex Bender

Published by:
The Extraordinary Girl, LLC
Carbondale, CO

ISBN 978-0615-42978-6

First Edition
Printed in the United States of America

My father used to sing Perry Como's "A You're Adorable" to me when I was a little girl. He also shared it with my three kids when they were small. He passed away in 2001, and this song reminds me of how much I miss him.

A you're adorable
B you're so beautiful
C you're a cutie full of charms
D you're a darling, and
E you're exciting
F you're a feather in my arms
G you look good to me
H you're so heavenly
I you're the one I idolize
J we're like Jack and Jill
K you're so kissable
L is the love light in your eyes
M, N, O, P, I could go on all day
Q, R, S, T, alphabetically speaking, you're OK
U made my life complete
V means you're very sweet
W, X, Y, Z
It's fun to wander through
The alphabet with you
To tell you what you mean to me

To borrow from this great song:

John, *I you're the one I idolize.*

This needs no further elaboration!

Mom, my siblings, and your families, *J we're like Jack and Jill.*

We're part of the same team, forever caring and helping each other. I can't imagine what it would be like to not have you all around.

Courtney and Tom, *A your adorable* and *B you're so beautiful.*

When I look at you both my heart melts, you are two of the most beautiful people I know. I'm so proud of you.

And to Alex, *U made my life complete.*

You've taught me compassion, caring, sensitivity and patience. I could wander through the alphabet with you and tell you what you mean to me, but there simply aren't enough letters to make my point.

Table of Contents

Introduction

My daughter, Alex, is a 17-year-old high school junior.

She's a singer and has performed on stage at local benefits. She's an actress who's been in the last three school plays. Alex is an artist with hundreds of pieces of art in her portfolio. She's my adventure girl, always up for a last-minute trip anywhere.

Alex loves sports, manages the boys high school football team and plays on the girls basketball and soccer teams. This past summer, she was one of 28 athletes chosen to represent the state of Colorado in the National Special Olympics Game held in Lincoln, NE., and earned a silver medal, as well as fifth-, sixth- and seventh- place finishes in track and field events.

Alex also has Down syndrome. Her math, reading and writing levels test in the third- to fifth-grade range. Her speech is intelligible, her sentences are generally made up of a maximum of ten words, and her grammar is correct about 75 percent of the time. She needs weekly speech therapy sessions to maintain and improve her language skills.

My husband and I battle with her about homework, eating habits and personal hygiene. Fortunately Alex is not apt to succumb to peer pressure like other teenagers, but the idea that she should study, eat healthy or dress like a 17-year- old girl are also not important to her. She'd prefer to be a ninja warrior.

Everyone who meets Alex falls in love with her. I would not change anything about her. Ever.

There is a wonderful piece called "Welcome to Holland" written by Emily Perl Kingsley, a mother of a child with special needs. It compares the birth of a child with special needs to being on a plane to Italy. You've always wanted to go to Italy and have waited a very long time, instead you land in Holland and are very disappointed. You never wanted to go to Holland.

In the spirit of this beautiful prose, I never imagined going to Holland. However, very quickly I learned Holland is just as beautiful as Italy, only different. Holland has tulips which is my favorite flower.

The Day that Rocked our World

Alex was born three weeks early on Saturday, June 19, 1993. She weighed less than 6 pounds and measured 17 petite and perfect inches. I fell in love with her at first sight.

Alex entered the world my favorite color, turquoise blue, her umbilical cord wrapped around her neck. Her Apgar score was low, so we only had a few moments with her until she was rushed to the neonatal intensive care unit (NICU) at the hospital. In the moments before she was whisked away, I saw that she had a partial head of black hair, ten beautiful fingers, ten beautiful toes, and the tiniest ears I had ever seen. My heart sank at the thought of her requiring extra medical care.

The doctor assured us she would be fine, but I didn't believe him, as the sound of the room going eerily quiet when Alex's head emerged from the birth canal still rang in my ears. In an attempt to suppress the fear rising up from my stomach, I asked the nurse if something was wrong. Her hesitation spoke much louder than her minimal words of comfort.

As soon as I could gather enough strength after the delivery, my husband John helped me shuffle down to the NICU. I felt a surge of adrenalin coupled with fear. Will Alex be okay? What's wrong with my perfect baby? Why did the mood in the delivery room resemble a funeral parlor instead of the party-like atmosphere that was present after the birth of my firstborn just 15 months earlier? It was a sense of dread I had never experienced.

My intuition took over as I asked to see the neonatal doctor, and what blurted out of my mouth surprised even me.

"Do you suspect Down syndrome?" I asked

Her reply was simple.

"Maybe. Have you seen her? We need to do a blood test and the results take three days."

That one "maybe" changed our world forever. We left the NICU feeling deflated, defeated and cheated. Down syndrome was the most awful thing we could ever imagine. But I had already fallen in love with Alex and could not reconcile that my perfect baby, who had already become part of my soul, had Down syndrome.

Three days later, the results came back positive for Down syndrome. John and I had already accepted that the initial diagnosis was correct, but our family had held out hope that the doctors were wrong. Thus began our extraordinary journey of learning to embrace Down syndrome, and after a period of realization that this much awaited and eagerly anticipated baby had Down syndrome, our families joined us every step of the way.

To this day, I believe when Alex was delivered, the nurse immediately recognized she had Down syndrome, while the delivery doctor did not. The doctor had read and blindly accepted the results of the prenatal tests on my chart suggesting we were having a normal (an often misused term) baby.

I was 34 when I delivered my first daughter, Courtney, and although Alex came along less than a year and a half later, in that time I had graduated to the high-risk "older mothers" category, which prompts the medical community to recommend more in depth tests for birth defects and other genetic abnormalities. I agreed to undergo the CVS test, which can be done very early in the pregnancy by inserting a needle unceremoniously and uncomfortably through the vagina in search of fetal cells. By culturing the extracted cells, the geneticists can count the baby's chromosomes and look for unusual genetic markers.

It takes 10 days to receive the results, and mine came back as failed because no fetal cells had been collected, which only happens once in about every 10,000 tests or so. The wait had been riddled with anxiety, as well as an increased risk of spontaneous miscarriage, so I opted to forgo a second test.

The doctor then suggested I submit to an amniocentesis, which is performed later in the pregnancy. For me, it was around the time I felt bonded with my baby, having felt tiny kicks from the womb. As a needle was rudely being inserted into my abdomen, I mentioned I was en route to the airport. The doctor quickly pulled the needle out and refused to do the test. Apparently, the hole that would be created in the amniotic sac would be more likely to rupture in the low pressure of an airplane and cause a miscarriage. Instead, he did a full ultrasound and declared my baby perfect. I left for my vacation happy and confident about the little being I was carrying.

These unlikely slip-ups of the professionals entrusted to watch over our unborn child gave me — us — the incredible opportunity to not have to make a decision I would have spent my life regretting. I had two failed attempts to learn my baby had Down syndrome. I thank the universe daily for saving me from having to make a decision about whether to terminate my pregnancy. I never had to call my family for advice that might have prevented me from meeting Alex. Nor did I ever have the chance to see a baby with Down syndrome and wonder, "What if?"

Every day countless women are presented with information that affects their pregnancies. I don't judge another woman's decision relative to her life and family. I'm just glad I never faced that very complex choice. Our family, friends and the world would have never known the magic of Alex. She has changed us all.

I'm often told I am a great mom because I have a child with Down syndrome, although I would simply argue that I'm just like any other mom of three except that one of them happens to have Down syndrome. I do agree our family life is a bit different, as we have grown in a way I have never imagined we would or could. Alex has enriched our lives in a way very few people ever experience.

We've learned compassion, caring, and acceptance under uncommon circumstances. We've met incredible families who have children with special needs, as well as many adults with special needs. We've worked with caring and skilled professionals. Our family feels honored to have had this opportunity.

These past 17 years have been an unexpected and beautiful adventure. As with many unplanned journeys, stages must be traveled before acceptance is embraced. I'm sharing our experience with the hope that the story of our voyage will help other families who have been touched by Down syndrome.

I've come to know our experience in terms of 10 verbs (as well as one bonus verb). The first four were John's and mine; the last six belong to all of us — John and me, and Alex, Courtney and our youngest Tom.

1. Grieve
2. Research
3. Incorporate
4. Promote
5. Include
6. Understand
7. Advocate
8. Expect the best
9. Practice healthy skepticism
10. Plan
Bonus: Celebrate

It's my sincere hope that by sharing our story, others will come to embrace theirs, or learn of the similar journey traveled by hundreds of thousands of people across the world.

From Grief to Celebration

VERB 1: Grieve

Grief is a natural process usually associated with death, but I believe for us it was an effective and healthy way to learn to accept and embrace the unexpected. We didn't know Alex had Down syndrome, nor did we know very much about it. A period of grief and adjustment proved to be necessary for my husband, family and me. Finding the strength to grieve was my first lesson of Down syndrome, and perhaps one of the most important.

In the first few hours and days after Alex's birth and her unexpected diagnosis, it was about us and the "why?" and "how?" Why did Alex have Down syndrome? Why did *this* happen to *us*? How can we tell our families, who were overjoyed at the prospect of another baby, that ours was different? How do we share our sadness without seeming ungrateful and still put on a happy face? Why me, why us, why Alex, was all I could think about through my tears of sadness.

Although I always tried to keep my happy face on, I felt like a failure and was in a state of disbelief that I had created a "flawed" baby. I was embarrassed, humiliated and ashamed and didn't want to tell my parents or in-laws for fear I would somehow be blamed for having a baby with Down syndrome. I didn't want anyone to know that in most cases, the extra chromosome comes from the mother. I convinced myself I had let down my husband, my 15-month-old daughter and my family. I was scared to death and angry at the world. I was ignorant.

I tried to blame anyone and everyone. Perhaps there was a slight chance it was John who contributed the extra chromosome. Maybe I lived in an area with tainted water, or unusual electricity. Maybe the tests results were wrong. My mind invented reasons to explain Alex, and although I loved her immediately, I selfishly hoped her Down syndrome would just go away.

I obsessed about science. Couldn't someone create a magical organism that ate the 47th chromosome in each of Alex's cells? Why wasn't there a cure for Down syndrome? My imagination grew wild with ideas about how to "fix" Alex. What a waste of time.

The professionals we spoke with explained a lot about Down syndrome and quieted my overly active mind. I remember one pediatrician came into my room at the hospital and asked if I knew anything about it. I recall saying that all I knew was "they all looked alike." He was horrified and said that was akin to saying all white people looked alike. I felt like I had been slapped and vowed at that moment to never make gross generalizations again.

Many couples grieve apart from each other, and my husband and I hear stories of marriages crumbling as a result of the birth of a child with special needs. John and I have been able to stay together, but we've had our differences and up and downs. We often disagree on Alex's education or the appropriate punishment for bad behavior, but we often find a compromise, as I believe we're both always partially right. John would say that we both needed to grieve separately before we could grieve together, and I wholeheartedly agree. Although we were together physically, I know for the few weeks following Alex's birth, we were apart emotionally.

I cried, cried and cried some more. I remember after visiting Alex in the hospital, as she stayed and I was released, John and I sat outside the entrance to Lutheran General Hospital in Park Ridge, IL, and cried so hard we shook. I didn't care that we were in a public place, the sadness we felt was uncontrollable. It was the last time we ever cried together about our grief for ourselves, or for the birth of Down syndrome in our lives.

My tears lasted for a month and a half. I spent hours driving around aimlessly in my car, sometimes with Alex, often by myself. On one of those first rides I heard Louis Armstrong's "What a Wonderful World." It moved me and I went out and bought the CD so I could listen to it over and over again. The words helped heal me.

I see trees of green, red roses too
I see them bloom for me and you
And I think to myself what a wonderful world.

I vividly remember the six-week appointment with my OB/GYN after Alex was born. The doctor, who was not the one who delivered Alex, asked how I was doing. Choked by my tears, I was unable to respond. When I finally blurted out that she had Down syndrome, the doctor looked at me and asked, "Is she healthy?" That was all he cared about, and, I realized, all I really needed to care about, too.

During Alex's hospital stay in the NICU, she was seen by a cardiologist, gastrointestinal specialist, audiologist, and optometrist, among others. A geneticist, social worker and a doctor who specialized in working with children with Down syndrome saw John and me. Meeting with these professionals was part of our healing process. It was also the beginning of our transition into the next verb: Research.

Alex was given a clean bill of health, with the exception of some minor heart issues, which are very common in children with Down syndrome. The condition actually turned out to be fortuitous, as we saw the cardiologist every six months and a condition not common in children with Down syndrome was discovered at 21 months, and Alex had surgery for coarctation of the aorta repair.

John, who loves being outside and carries all of his serious thoughts inside his figurative backpack on walks and hikes, was devastated when Alex was diagnosed with Down syndrome. He spent hours in the outdoors adjusting to a life he never expected, a future he never dreamed of. But those walks helped him heal, and he says he never looked back.

In hindsight, he says he was ignorant. Just like me he had no idea what Down syndrome was and why it had become part of our lives. My husband is not the type of person who blames others for unexplained and unexpected events in his life. But in this case he may have blamed me, I don't know. I'll never ask him, as it doesn't really matter now, and even if he did, I know today he'd thank me for bringing Alex into our lives.

On a more practical note, we also had to talk to our families. This shift from lack of action to tactical movement was a huge step in our ability to grieve and move forward. As Alex remained in the hospital for five days after her birth it gave us some of the time we needed to get our emotional house in order.

John and I took a brief moment to digest the idea of a different life — more different than how we assumed it would be by simply bringing a second child into the world — as well as share the news with our families and closest friends. Fortunately, everyone met us with support and unconditional love. My parents, who lived 2,000 miles away, insisted my mom arrive on the next plane, and she did. My brother-in-law and sister-in-law along with their four children, who lived in our town, became the head cheerleaders in the "welcome to the world" celebration.

When Courtney was born we sent out 150 birth announcements, and I wanted to do the same to celebrate Alex's birth. However, I didn't know how I wanted to share our news with my friends to whom I couldn't speak, as well as others. We decided to enclose a letter along with the birth announcement - and it, too, helped us heal.

July 8, 1993

Dear Friends and Family,

On June 19 John & I were very happy to experience the birth of our second child and daughter, Alex. Alex has Down syndrome, which took us completely by surprise. My pregnancy had been uneventful and every indicator was normal.

Fortunately for us, I delivered Alex in a hospital with an excellent reputation for treating newborns with all sorts of problems. As Down syndrome was suspected by the doctors shortly after Alex's birth, she was tested for the most common physical problems affecting Down's children. This included heart, lung and lower GI tract problems. Her muscle tone was also checked and her ability to feed and digest her food. Happily, she passed all of her testing with flying colors.

Although we were heartbroken at first, we have realized that first Alex is a baby, and secondly she has Down syndrome. Not the other way around. We didn't plan for this but we are preparing for it.

We are now semi-experts on Down syndrome and are learning about all the programs that are available to Alex so she will be able to reach her highest potential. This involves something called early intervention where she will be able to work with therapists to help her develop the skills she will need to be able to go to school and function as a normal child. Alex will receive the best care we can give her.

Alex is active, alert, cute and we love her. We hope you will all get a chance to meet her. I expect we will all become better people for having Alex in our lives.

Love, Gary & John

We received enough loving and supportive responses to fill a shoebox, and then some. The stories of other children with Down syndrome shared by family and friends — a mixture of happy, sad and promising — were the medicine we needed.

Through our first few hours, days and weeks of Alex, we quickly gained a great deal of knowledge and insight. We learned grieving was important; we needed to adjust. We also learned having a child with Down syndrome was not the end of the world. It didn't make us different in a bad way, but it undoubtedly made us different. We learned our friends and family would always be there for us, no matter what, which was a blessing and something I had never appreciated previously. We continue to learn how fortunate we are to enjoy that kind of support. I wish it for everyone.

However, not all new families have the needed support, and these families must actively search for others to help them through the grieving process. Finding emotional assistance as quickly as possible is critical, as oftentimes grief cannot be handled effectively if done silently or alone. Down syndrome can bring magic to your life, but finding where it's hiding without the help of others can be an excruciating process.

I now know that all of the reactions we had are not uncommon for new parents of children with Down syndrome. I don't pretend to know the answers. However, once we got to know Alex and felt instinctively that she was just like her sister in so many ways, we subconsciously shifted from grief about ourselves to grief about and for Alex.

We've also learned that when Alex was born we didn't mourn only for ourselves but also for Alex's future and ours. Would she ever learn to read? Would she be able to speak? Would she be able to go to school, play sports and have friends? Would she ever be accepted? Would she ever get married? Would she be able to move out of our house? Would she have a relationship with her sister like I did with mine? What would the future bring?

The same thoughts still swirl around in my head, particularly since Alex will graduate from high school next year. But these are no longer borne from grief, but from love. I love Alex and her siblings so much and dream of a future of success for all three — success in relationships and professional and personal pursuits.

Grief moved us through the transition from sorrow to love, helped us accept the things we cannot change, and put us on the path to find the strength to change the things we can.

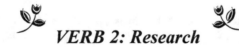

VERB 2: Research

As soon as possible after we learned Alex had Down syndrome, we began our research. We didn't know anything about it, and the unknown was terrifying. In hindsight, I recognize the research we undertook was one of the many factors that moved us out of our grieving phase. The more we learned, the more I realized our lives would be fine — just like everyone else's, only different.

The first thing we learned was that the technical name for Down syndrome is Trisomy 21, which means an extra chromosome exists in the 21st set of genes. This gene "overcodes" and trumps many other attributes, including intelligence, muscle tone and physical features. It causes mild to severe delays in speech, cognitive learning and gross and fine motor skills. Additionally, many children with Down syndrome have serious medical issues that must be addressed at birth or soon after. We were lucky — maybe it goes back to the one in 10,000 chance of a failed CVS test — but Alex has had only minor health issues in her 17 years.

In 1993, the Internet wasn't terribly advanced, so we resorted to more traditional forms of knowledge: books and people. Seventeen years ago I didn't know too much about Down syndrome and what I thought I knew turned out to be false, pre-conceived ideas. Reading books on the subject was a lifesaver.

Babies With Down syndrome: A New Parent's Guide (The Special-Needs Collection) (Woodbine House, Inc., 1992)

I bought 20 copies and distributed them to everyone in our extended families. My father was one of the first to read the book, which I knew instantly from his newly enlightened demeanor.

Where's Chimpy? (Albert Whitman Concept Paperbacks, 1991)

As young parents, we were always reminded to read to our children. This book was Alex's favorite. My goal was to have the words "Down syndrome" become part of our vernacular. This book was enjoyable to Alex, and I could talk about the little girl with Down syndrome while reading it to her.

Our Brother Has Down's Syndrome (Annick Press, Ltd., 1985)

This is the book Alex and I read to her first- and second-grade classes. After reading it we engaged her classmates in a question-and-answer session, which was useful in helping them understand Alex was just like them, only a little different.

Teaching Reading to Children With Down Syndrome: A Guide for Parents and Teachers (Topics in Down syndrome) (Woodbine House, Inc., 1995)

When Alex started school, I found this book, which I purchased for her teachers. I know at least some of them read it as we discussed learning strategies in her early team meetings.

A recent search on Amazon.com also turned up links to these books:

Communication Skills in Children With Down Syndrome: A Guide for Parents (Topics in Down syndrome) (Woodbine House, Inc., 1995)

Teaching Math to People With Down Syndrome and Other Hands-On Learners: Basic Survival Skills (Topics in Down syndrome) Book 1 (Woodbine House, Inc., 2004)

Gross Motor Skills in Children With Down Syndrome: A Guide for Parents and Professionals (Topics in Down syndrome) (Woodbine House, Inc., 1997)

Fine Motor Skills for Children With Down Syndrome: A Guide for Parents And Professionals (Topics in Down syndrome) (Woodbine House, Inc., 2006)

I was also able to enjoy a few inspirational books and know there are now many more available; I really should update my personal library.

Expecting Adam: A True Story of Birth, Rebirth, and Everyday Magic (Times Books, a division of Random House, Inc., 1999)

Count Us In: Growing Up with Down Syndrome (A Harvest Book) (Harcourt, Inc. 1994)

As Alex gets older and nutrition and sexuality are becoming very important to her and to us, these books are on my list:

The Down Syndrome Nutrition Handbook: A Guide to Promoting Healthy Lifestyles (Phronesis Publishing, LLC, 2006)

Teaching Children with Down Syndrome about Their Bodies, Boundaries, and Sexuality (Woodbine House Inc., 2007)

Families looking for resources should also consider the abundance of online support groups, Down syndrome sites and blogs. A simple Google search brings up millions of links to sites rich with information like local, statewide and international support groups, professional Down syndrome organizations, national and international studies on medical advances and research, and blogs that can be used as support and reference tools.

As much as I love and use the Internet now, I still believe there's nothing more important to a new parent of a child with special needs than a face-to-face meeting or phone conversation; it provides an interactive and open forum that I have not found anywhere, except perhaps in the blogging community.

It seems everyone knows someone you should talk to when an extraordinary life event unfolds. I'm not the type to make cold calls on someone's suggestion, but after Alex's birth, I wasn't shy. I got the names of a number of local families who had children with Down syndrome. It surprised me just how many families there were, as we lived in a small community and I had never met any of them. I have since learned the Down syndrome community is large — there are more than 400,000 people in the United States with Down syndrome. Alex is not unusual at all.

After speaking with three families, I began to notice a pattern to our conversations and heard the same thing repeatedly:

"Alex will bring sunshine to your life."

"Alex will make you a better person."

"Alex will enrich your lives in ways you never knew existed."

"Alex will lead a full life."

It was as if these parents all drank a magic potion that caused them to say the same thing. I didn't believe for a second they were right. But within six months I learned I was wrong, more wrong than I had ever been. I guzzled that magic potion and can now say those words as fast as I can say my own name.

Understanding as quickly as possible what our future looked like was a relief. It was almost as if the clouds of grief became rays of sunshine.

From Grief to Celebration

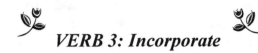

VERB 3: Incorporate

Research helped us understand Down syndrome, and that children and adults with Down syndrome can and will lead fulfilling lives. The future for our special children is bright; education and job training are available to help people with Down syndrome succeed. In most ways, the misconceptions of previous generations are disappearing and society has become much more accepting and inclusive of people of many disabilities.

We realized very early on that Alex and Down syndrome would be in our lives forever, so we unconsciously began to incorporate it into our lives. After saying "Alex has Down syndrome" a few times it became easier and less scary and was fully integrated into conversations with and about our family.

We told everyone we knew that Alex had Down syndrome, and we didn't make it a big deal. We reconciled that this was a normal event in our family's life about which we were neither sad nor upset. It was almost like we were saying Alex had green eyes and brown hair; to us, Down syndrome became a part of who she was, and who we were. We were armed with research whenever friends or family requested additional information, but as people got to know Alex, it became a non-event.

If I called a babysitter, I would mention Alex had Down syndrome. If I enrolled in a Mommy and Me class, I also brought it to their attention. I made sure any new health care providers we saw knew Alex had Down syndrome before we walked into their office. I never had any pushback or hesitation from anyone who cared for our kids. It was an easy transition and we embraced these two new words in our language. Today I still shout it from the rooftops: DOWN SYNDROME!

Although she was only 15 months old, we also told Courtney about Alex and used the term Down syndrome a lot in our house. I don't think Courtney ever thought it was strange or weird; her sister simply has Down syndrome. But for a child with a sibling with disabilities, it's not always easy. Last year, as Courtney was filling out applications for college, she shared her entrance essay with me:

It is easier to rip a newspaper along the grains. There, the paper is uniform and the tear is clear. I had envisioned my life to be along the grain. I wanted to be the same as everyone else. My school, my clothes, and my music resembled everyone else's in my grade. My family, however, didn't.

In 1st grade I realized my sister was different. This meant that I was different through association. Alex will only ever be as smart as a middle school student-her standardized tests scores can attest to that. I have a sister who won't be able to live on her own.

School was mine. I entered the decorated classroom and forgot my family at home. I had new friends and they were the social group of the grade. What eight-year-old kid doesn't want to be the center of attention? As far as anyone was concerned, I was just like everyone else.

But I really wasn't. My sister called for me from across crowded hallways and across the congested playground every day. Eyes would turn to me, wondering how I was going to react. When I heard her, I turned the other way and didn't respond. My cheeks would burn and I wondered what people were thinking. I wanted to get away from her and I couldn't. She was always the next bedroom away.

Eventually, I stopped trying to live my life in the control seat. I stopped living my own life in general. People saw me through my sister, so that is what I became- Alex's sister. I sat in the corner while she was out talking to people and singing her off-key songs. I became what I thought people perceived me as. I was quiet and reserved, and I gave center stage to my sister.

I don't remember exactly when I realized that I didn't have to be second to her. Alex participates in a lot of activities for children with disabilities, one being therapeutic horseback riding. I spent a lot of time with my sister at her horseback riding sessions, where I watched her confidence grow and her fear become insignificant. She was a real person, and could handle herself well. Who was this girl that caused me so much grief? Did I make her up?

The newspaper was ripped, and there was no going back. I took another look at my life. I saw my sister as a girl who, yes, loves to be the center of attention, but at the same time grew as a real person. She wasn't afraid to be herself around new people, or around friends. What I ran from in school wasn't my sister, but it was the idea of a child with Down Syndrome, a child who's different. It was unnecessary energy that I put into hiding from her that I should have spent understanding my sister.

Every weekend, I watch Alex as she jumps out of the car before I turn off the engine. Watching her makes me warm even on the coldest winter days. I love my sister as a person, and through our differences, I've come to realize she has helped shape the person I am. My friends aren't along the grain, they are far from it, and I love them for always being themselves. By keeping my world open to opportunity, I've stopping looking at how far I've deviated since elementary school and have come to realize how close my life is to the one I've always wanted.

Tom, who was born when Alex was a little more than two years old, also knew his sister was different, but he never questioned why. I know he sometimes wishes Alex wasn't in his life, but to be fair, he wishes that of Courtney, too. Alex can be very mean to Tom, but he takes it well, never retaliating or picking a fight. He knows he'll end up the victor in any verbal or physical match and proving his superiority over Alex is not important to him. He doesn't feel sorry for Alex, but accepts her for who she is and doesn't judge her for what she has.

In Tom's words:

Alex is one of the meanest people to me that I know. She consistently tells me that she hates me and to "go away" or "leave now," or asks me every time I look at her "what do you want?" But there are always those days, which are becoming more common, when she is nice to me. Where she says that she loves me and accepts my hug. Alex cries a lot, sometimes for good reasons or sometimes for almost no reason at all. I do understand that Alex has a different way of interpreting things than most people. Overall I am becoming more and more happy to have a sister like Alex. My life would have been way different without Alex

John and I are proud that Courtney and Tom have become outspoken advocates of all children with challenges and are often cited by teachers as great examples to the other students. By incorporating Down syndrome into the lives of Courtney and Tom, we unknowingly (but very happily) created a different future for them.

Courtney is majoring in molecular engineering in college. The whole idea of the extra chromosome has always fascinated her, which in turn sparked an insatiable interest in science. Tom is a sophomore in high school and spends some of his free time as a volunteer for organizations that provide services to children and adults with disabilities. I'm so amazed at the people my children are becoming, which is something I also hear repeatedly from other families that have children with Down syndrome.

By incorporating Down syndrome into the normalcy of our lives, we were able to move along on our path to acceptance. It is who we are, the family with a child with Down syndrome. I am proud of all of us.

VERB 4: Promote

When Alex was still in the hospital after her birth, a social worker visited John and me. She was employed by the hospital and her responsibilities included providing information to parents of newborns with special needs. Pre-Internet, the only real way to do research was through bookstores, libraries and phone calls. Since we were in a hospital with little access to reading material, we had a huge number of questions. The social worker was able to answer some of them. For what she didn't know, she referred us to an organization called the National Association for Down Syndrome (NADS).

From that day until we left the Chicago area in 2006, NADS became the most important resource in our life. NADS is a Chicago-based not-for-profit that provides support for individuals with Down syndrome and their families. According to its website:

NADS is the oldest organization in the country serving individuals with Down syndrome and their families. It was founded in Chicago in 1961 by parents who chose to go against medical advice and raised their children with Down syndrome at home. Their pioneering efforts have made it easier for later generations of individuals with Down syndrome to be accepted by their families and communities, to develop their capabilities, and to work towards independence. Our mission is to ensure that all persons with Down syndrome have the opportunity to achieve their potential in all aspects of community life. We offer information, support, and advocacy.

I called their office immediately and received a call back from Sheila, the Executive Director. Under the care of a nurturing doctor, Sheila took Christopher, her baby son with Down syndrome, home from the hospital in the mid '70s. This was quite unusual in an era in which doctors were still recommending institutionalizing children with Down syndrome. Christopher is a remarkable young man who plays piano skillfully, enjoys an active social life and works full time.

These are the parents of older children with Down syndrome from across the entire country who paved the way for the babies of the '80s, '90s and the 21st century. Never does a doctor recommend institutionalization to today's parents. Every day I'm grateful to Sheila and these parents of earlier generations who loved their babies unconditionally, brought them home and began the battle for services and education that are given without hesitation today. Of course funding remains an issue with our schools and other providers, but at least our battle isn't borne from a lack of knowledge, compassion and understanding of others.

Sheila immediately assured me — and was the first person to do so — that Alex would have a full and complete life.

Her exact words were, "Remember, she is a baby first," which was something I needed to hear.

She also told me of the school resources that were available immediately. Sheila gave us a ton of information, sending us on our path as advocates, promoters and supporters of our special daughter armed with every piece of equipment and knowledge we never knew we needed.

I subsequently became involved with NADS as a volunteer. John and I were support parents and were called upon to visit new families with babies with Down syndrome in our area. We visited parents at home, in the hospital and talked to others on the phone. We shared our experience, but recognized many of these parents were grieving. **I became one of those parents who had told me everything would be fine.** We had drunk the magic potion, incorporated Down syndrome into our lives and graduated to promoting it.

We listened and answered questions, and knew we could help but not solve, just as our own experience had shown. It was an incredible feeling to help these young families, just as others helped us. We really learned what it means to pay it forward. I try to do this every day of my life.

I also became a mentor to an adult with Down syndrome, and today I still stay in touch with Cindy by e-mail. She lives in a supervised apartment with two other adults with disabilities and works at her local grocery store. She also participates in the Special Olympics and is a huge supporter of Alex and her accomplishments. Cindy opened my eyes to her extraordinary life, which is full of friends and happiness.

Being a part of NADS, an organization devoted to education, inclusion and acceptance, was unbelievably fulfilling. We will always promote and share our experiences with Down syndrome at every available opportunity. In some ways, we're like evangelists, proudly and passionately spreading the message of Down syndrome wherever we go, both by our words and deeds.

By learning to promote Down syndrome we learned so much more from others. We embraced NADS and met so many people similar to us. Parents who were grieving, parents who were researching and parents who were celebrating. Promote was a verb we needed to accept, and it changed our lives once we did.

VERB 5: Include

The next six verbs were the actions that became an integral part of the fabric of our family. John and I no longer needed to reconcile Alex's diagnosis of Down syndrome as parents because our family embraced it so fully. It became part of who we are.

We found that by actively seeking opportunities to include Alex, whether they were art lessons, sports teams or school, what we were really doing was tackling Alex's special needs. We made her part of our community and, more importantly, ensured we were part of hers. We believed and insisted she was no longer the kid with Down syndrome; rather she was a kid who happened to have Down syndrome.

Our first experience in including Alex in a community, albeit the special needs community, began three weeks after she was born. Our school district had a now-defunct program called PIE in which other moms with kids with special needs between the ages of six months and three years old met once a week in a classroom for a kind of playgroup. Activities included speech, occupational and physical therapists, as well as an early childhood educator.

I believe that early services, or early intervention, are critical for all children with special needs. There are countless stories and studies that prove the value. I've seen and heard of children who were born in the '40s and '50s who were either institutionalized or kept in seclusion in their homes. We can compare these babies as adults to those children who were brought home from the hospital, educated and had their issues addressed early on — mostly by their parents and siblings. This action guaranteed their success, and many of these adults with disabilities are now active members of our communities. I'm so grateful to all of the rogue and brave parents who paved the way for us.

Once a week is certainly not enough time to provide all the necessary services, but it served as a tremendous foundation. The moms were able to share information and support, which is crucial to parents of babies with disabilities. We were able to get thoughts and ideas on our children's strengths and weaknesses from professionals. I knew very early on that we needed to concentrate on Alex's muscle tone, although only a little bit, as her muscle tone was high compared to others with Down syndrome. But while her strength would come, we did need to focus on her speech.

To that end, we worked with a private speech therapist and learned sign language. Signing was a miracle, as it turns out. Children with Down syndrome do form language in their minds, but their speech is generally very delayed, as they have difficulty transferring it to understandable sounds.

The theory behind signing is kids will gain confidence and accelerate their speech when they learn that their families can understand their needs. Alex was able to make simple signs for "more," "play," and "drink" at 11 months old. Communicating was gratifying for all of us. She spoke her first words at 15 months and her real sentences came at age three. However, speech is still a huge issue for us. We're certainly able to understand Alex and she does speak in full sentences, but without constant reinforcement she regresses. This skill, so simple to so many, is one of the most important tools Alex has. She can communicate with us and her peers. Without basic language skills, many children are excluded from social interactions, which is the most important step in inclusion.

It makes sense to prepare our special children for the world as soon as possible so they can be active and contributing members of society. After all, it's what we do for our "normal" kids.

The next step in working towards inclusion is through the individualized education plan or program (IEP). The IEP is one of the many tools that educators and parents use to educate a child with special needs, as well as prepare the child to become a fully integrated member of the community. This plan of education is conceived by a team of educators as well as the parents. When used correctly, it's a fabulous tool.

The IEP is generated when the child enters the public school system, which was age six in Alex's case. Additionally, a special education determination must be made. Fortunately for a child with Down syndrome, special education eligibility is determined at birth by federal law. This translates into school districts that are mandated to educate our kids, for whom we never had to fight for service eligibility. However, in today's economic climate, we have to fight for service providers.

Our team put Alex's plan together just before she started kindergarten. We wove inclusion into every aspect of her goals, but also recognized situations where she would be better served in a resource, or special education room.

As I understand it, the IDEA (Individuals with Disabilities Education Act) which was revamped and passed in 2004 requires this IEP must be written according to the needs of each student who meets eligibility and must utilize guidelines under the IDEA and state regulations. It can be very formal, but is an excellent framework for education of our special kids.

As everyone I know has had a different IEP experience, I find this excerpt from the United States Department of Education helpful in explaining the idea:

The term individualized education program or IEP means a written statement for each child with a disability that is developed, reviewed, and revised in a meeting in accordance with must include:

- *A statement of the child's present levels of academic achievement and functional performance.*
- *A statement of measurable annual goals, including academic and functional goals designed to:*
  - *Meet the child's needs that result from the child's disability to enable the child to be involved in and make progress in the general education curriculum; and*
  - *Meet each of the child's other educational needs that result from the child's disability;*
- *For children with disabilities who take alternate assessments aligned to alternate achievement standards, a description of benchmarks or short-term objectives*

- *A description of*
  - *How the child's progress toward meeting the annual goals will be measured; and*
  - *When periodic reports on the progress the child is making toward meeting the annual goals (such as through the use of quarterly or other periodic reports, concurrent with the issuance of report cards) will be provide;*

The IEP becomes the bible that parents and educators use throughout the child's educational experience, which can last until age 21. In theory, it's a successful strategy. I wholeheartedly embraced Alex's IEP as well as our multi-disciplinary team.

We saw and still see weekly or monthly improvements in language, reading, math and general cognitive abilities. Alex and most children with Down syndrome learn extremely well when they don't feel excluded from their peers. I've found that peer competition and the desire to keep up with her peers, is the best way for Alex to learn.

I often meet parents of younger children with Down syndrome who tell me they think Alex is doing well. I have three responses: 1) early intervention, 2) inclusion, and 3) a supportive school district. I know school districts obviously vary from area to area, and certainly funding cuts have affected services. My advice: persevere and insist!

At the same time, however, I also struggle with my own philosophy. I did, and still do, support inclusion. I believe that Alex benefits from being included in as many academic and social situations as possible, and that others benefit from her presence and participation as well. Oftentimes parents and kids relay to me how Alex has changed their lives and opened their eyes to new things in the world. This is also good for Alex, as she uses these experiences to model her behaviors. I don't believe in segregating Alex from her peers, but I do believe a blend of both worlds is successful for Alex.

What I didn't believe at the time, but know now, is that Alex shines when she's with other people with disabilities. She can interact equally, both socially and competitively. She feels genuine friendship, pride and success. As the mother of a child with disabilities, it's rewarding to see your child so happy, particularly since there are struggles in other parts of her life.

The Special Olympics was the answer for us. It's very difficult to find the words to describe how much the Special Olympics have meant to our family. Her coaches are professional, yet empathic and caring. They don't tolerate some of the behaviors that I know Alex gets away with at school. Both of her coaches treat each and every kid as an athlete first, and then if needed, as an athlete who may need accommodations.

In the Special Olympics, Alex is an unequivocal star. She displays impressive coordination and often places first or second during the Summer and Fall State Olympic Games. Her team of eight to ten athletes supports and encourages each other. It's one of the few places in her life where Alex is a respected leader.

Inclusion is critical, especially for younger kids who learn by example and from their peers. However, as a mom of a daughter with Down syndrome, I also want Alex to succeed on a more level playing field. And as she has gotten older and her delays relative to her peers have become more pronounced, this blend has worked for Alex.

Inclusion, segregation and integration are only words; practicing what we preach will make all the difference.

From Grief to Celebration

VERB 6: *Understand*

"Understand" has two entirely different applications for a family with a child with special needs. We need to understand our children, and, at the same time, understand others and their frame of reference about Down syndrome.

We try to practice the "put yourself in their shoes" rule most of the time, but our success rate is unfortunately not 100 percent, although it's not that far off.

Understand Alex

There are two critical parts to understanding Alex: her behavior and speech. Her behavior is directly related to how she feels about herself, and her occasional acts of frustration are an extended result. I still don't know exactly what makes the thoughts in her brain connect, but I do know they bond at a different speed than mine.

I'm always trying to figure out what makes Alex tick, what I can do to help her master a new skill and how I can help her make sense of something. I often need to remind myself that she is different than me, as well as my other kids. I try to put myself in her shoes, even though I know her methods and ways will likely puzzle me for years to come. Regardless, she is entitled to all the same privileges enjoyed by any child.

When my father-in-law died last year, I had no idea how Alex would process the grief. As it turns out, her behavior took a steep downhill turn. She became stubborn, rude and inconsolable. A year later she mentions grandpa with a smile, but she can also cry when we share a memory about him.

Alex had a deep connection with her grandpa. Their bond was evident early on; she gravitated towards him and he to her. There was a twinkle in his eye when she was with him, and she no doubt felt his unconditional love. He joked with her, but wouldn't tolerate her if she was rude.

Grandpa loved to play cards, and Alex loves to change the game rules so she wins. Grandpa cooperated (albeit a bit confused at times with her ever-changing instructions) and lost many a card game, but always with a wink and a smile.

I wasn't sure how Alex would express her sorrow, or even if she'd be able to act appropriately at the funeral service since she hadn't quite experienced this kind of loss before. She cried harder than most of us, particularly at the cemetery. She also laughed the loudest and smiled the most when we gathered with her cousins and cousins' children.

But her grief became most apparent as we traveled back home and she had an epic meltdown in the middle of the airport. Although tantrums in public places were commonplace for all of my kids when they were little, I hadn't experienced one in 12 years. Trying to understand Alex's sadness and delayed processing helped me handle the situation in a somewhat rational way.

As Alex screamed at me, "I hate you! I am not going home!", I became the center of attention, the other travelers staring at me with pity. I quickly told Tom and Courtney to get on the plane so they could be spared from the embarrassment.

Sometimes reason works with Alex, but logic didn't stop her from missing her grandpa, and I needed to put myself in her head. I quietly asked Alex to follow me on the plane, which is also what I told her that her grandpa would have wanted her to do. I also used Alex's logic and took her Nintendo with me. It took her a while, but eventually she followed me. It was ugly, and painful, but I recognize it's part of the process, and I really do understand.

As we arrived home, Alex looked at me with her adorable face and charming smile and said, "Tough day, Mom." All I could do was laugh and hope that was as tough as it gets.

Speech is difficult for many people with Down syndrome. Like when Alex used sign language as an infant, she still knows what she wants to say, but getting her brain and her mouth to coordinate can be a challenge. I believe that the clearer the diction and the better constructed Alex's sentences are, the less prejudice she's likely to encounter. It's unfortunate but true that too often a person's language abilities are subconscious indicators to others of cognitive abilities.

If people understand Alex and she can hold her own in a conversation, it will generally be assumed she's bright. It may not be the case in all situations, but I feel if you start from a place of acceptance, you'll be better off in the long run. As far as speech goes, my mantra is speech therapy, speech therapy and more speech therapy. It's one of the main soapboxes on which I stand when working with the school district.

Alex is very adept at compensating, which is something a very intuitive speech therapist helped her master. To this end, Alex has developed her own verbal expressions for when she's stuck. Most of these sayings are really good tactics to help her gather her thoughts, thereby giving her brain and mouth time to catch up. I find humor in her remarks and comments, but also try to understand her responses.

When Alex is confused about a question or unsure of an answer, she responds with one of the following:

"Good question. Let me think about it."

"I don't know. Can you ask me again?"

"I will check and get back to you."

When Alex feels pressured or is engaged in a conversation in which she perceives a negative energy, we often hear one of the following:

"I don't want to talk about it."

"I don't know. I told you this a hundred million times."

"Talk to the hand."

"You're weird."

When Alex is really upset (mostly at me), I hear:

"I don't want to be in this family anymore." (However, when I tell her she can join another family, she backs down.)

And my personal favorite, what I hear when I take Alex out to dinner or the movies:

"You are the best mother in the whole world!"

Alex has a response for everything, so many of which make us laugh and cry. She also has an uncanny ability to work the system. She loves to take time with her response when asked a question. Part of me thinks she needs to process the question, but part of John believes that Alex knows if she waits long enough, she creates an uncomfortable silence and someone else (mostly me) will answer for her. Once again, one of those disagreements we have about raising Alex. However, I believe John is probably right: Alex is mostly gentle and caring, but also manipulative and scheming at times, just like most other teenagers, including her siblings.

Understanding Others

It took me a really long time to understand how others perceived Alex — not with a lack of compassion, but from ignorance of Down syndrome. In my mind, ignorance can be addressed, and we try to educate the uninformed at every opportunity. Research, incorporate, promote and include all helped us to reach understanding, and it is the one verb I use every day unfailingly.

We've met many people through, or, I should say, because of Alex. Most of these people have been kind and supportive, but not everyone is, so I try to understand.

Following are the top 12 of many most irritating questions/statements I hear. I believe these comments are based on ignorance and I try to respond from that perspective, but sometimes it's harder than others.

I won't share my angry responses to these first five questions, as I am disappointed by my reactions, and I have learned to move on.

"Why should I teach her math? She can use a calculator."

"Why should I teach her to tie her shoes? There's Velcro."

"Why should I teach her to read beyond a third-grade level? She's going to live in assisted living anyway."

"Why does she need more speech therapy? She can talk."

"Can you come to the dance? Alex needs supervision."

I don't find the following questions offensive so much as misguided. My response to all of them is always, "Ask her."

"How old is she?"

"What's her name?"

"What school does she go to?"

"Does she have any brothers or sisters?"

The following three statements that I hear from time to time are meant to be compliments, but I find them to be untrue, which is why I'm sharing my unsaid responses.

"Only you and John could raise a child like Alex."

Sorry, we know lots of people that are raising children with special needs and they come from all walks of life. John and I are no different than any other parents. We love our children, no matter who they are, and we work to provide them all with the best future we can.

"God only gives you what you can handle."

Huh? What the heck does this even mean? We have a child with Down syndrome, that's the only difference between us and other families. I can argue that all kids can cause family angst.

"You're a great mother."

This is meant as a compliment, and I really do appreciate it, but it may or may not be true – only the future will tell. I know that I am no different than any other mother I know – so I guess that means we are all great mothers. The only difference is I have a daughter with Down syndrome.

I try to understand our current school district, which is under-resourced and underfunded. We work together to provide solutions for Alex that will not tax the special education teachers and providers more than they already are. But with this understanding I persevere and am usually happy with the solutions we generate.

I try to understand Alex's classmates and peers. Alex has grown a lot recently and has a much more mature view of peers and peer relationships. She recognizes that she doesn't have any true friends at school, merely 400 acquaintances. None of these acquaintances are girlfriends with whom she can talk or exchange genuine encouragement and appreciation. Teenage girls are mostly wrapped up in themselves. I try to understand they are not excluding Alex, they're just making sure they are included.

I try to find the humor in everything, which is usually easy. Mostly I try to understand and be thankful we have so many great people in our lives. Laugh is a verb I didn't include on my list, but maybe I should have.

From Grief to Celebration

VERB 7: Advocate

There are two ways in which we advocate for Alex. The first way is just that: very simply put, we advocate for Alex. The second — and more difficult — way is to teach Alex to advocate for herself (or self-advocate, in special education speak).

As soon as I found myself in the mainstream educational system, I recognized through my embrace of the verb understand that five- and six-year-olds and their parents didn't know Alex or even know anyone with Down syndrome. It was part of my responsibility as the parent of a very special daughter to advocate for her not only to her peers, but also to the school district. I discovered that the earlier her peers and school learned that I was an active advocate for my daughter, the easier it would be down the road.

I learned this again when we relocated to a different, less well-funded school district when Alex entered the seventh grade. It didn't take me long to realize I had to start advocating for Alex all over again. It has been challenging, and although we love where we live, I find myself advocating for Alex, her education and inclusion on a daily basis.

Don't get me wrong; this isn't a bad thing. I'm actually proud to set an example to other parents in our school district about being an advocate, as children with special needs are more of an anomaly in a rural area, and our schools have not been paying much attention to special education programs. I've made some progress, and even became one of the founding members of our area's Special Education Advisory Council (SEAC). Be sure to Google "SEAC" if you're not familiar with the concept.

My first acts of enthusiastic advocating occurred when Alex started first grade. I met with her teacher to talk about a success plan. One of my concerns from the beginning has been the other kids — how would they react to Alex, and would she be included in activities. I've always made it my business to meet with the teachers before school started to brainstorm various approaches. My teamwork method has always been well received, but due to funding issues, the resources necessary to create the team are overworked and over committed. Thinking outside the box has become status quo these days. I believe where there's a will, there's a way.

One of the things I did in first and second grade that worked well was meeting with Alex's class about a month after school started. As there were actually four classes in each grade, Alex and I met with two classes at a time. Our goal was to talk about Alex, demystify Down syndrome and answer questions. We started each session by reading "Our Brother Has Down's Syndrome" by Shelley Cairo. It's the story of a little boy with Down syndrome named Jai, as told by his sisters. It's easy to read and explains clearly that Jai is just like everyone else.

Alex and I sat at the front of the classroom, read the book, showed the pictures and stopped for questions along the way. We had practiced little sections for Alex to read so her classmates knew she was fully vested in our sessions, all of which were followed by a period of questions and answers.

It's fun to think back on those little kids, so excited to know Alex and meet her mom. First and second graders love to talk and share about themselves. I would ask them to share what was different about them, and learned many interesting family secrets, many of which I still remember (although my lips are sealed).

In the end, I believe the kids left with the message that Alex was more similar to them than they had previously imagined; she just has Down syndrome. She has brown hair and green eyes, went to the same school as they did, and loved to play sports. She does have an extra chromosome, and that's what makes her different. The kids loved learning about the chromosome that made Alex special.

Each year I sent a letter home to Alex's classmates' parents explaining the lesson I had taught and offering myself as a resource. Although I did get verbal feedback, it really was a non-event to everyone involved; Alex was Alex and part of the community. By the time I had read the book two years in a row, every kid in the school had heard the story at least once. The next four years were easy and although advocating is always important in terms of requesting services, it was never difficult.

Self-advocating is extremely important, and also very hard to teach. I believe Alex knows what she must do in terms of making her needs known as well as standing up for her rights. However, sometimes she simply doesn't have the confidence and tells me that others ignore her. As is the case with so many of her peers, while Alex demonstrates poise in other parts of her life, standing up for herself is more difficult.

When Alex feels self-assured, she succeeds in advocating for herself. Athletics is the perfect example. She plays high school soccer and basketball, as well as many Special Olympic sports. When she doesn't get enough play time in a basketball or a soccer game, she usually has no problem approaching the coaches. I believe this is because she knows her words provide immediate action. The coaches are generally responsive and listen to Alex. However, it isn't something that happened immediately or naturally. It took years of practice as well as our constant insistence before Alex handled her own problems.

I first understood Alex's ability to self-advocate at the end of her freshman year of high school. She decided she wanted to be on the boys football team. I could just hear her thinking, "What a great way to meet boys."

And with that, she self-advocated herself right on to that team. She approached the coach of the boys football team and told him she wanted to try out for the team. She gave him her father's business card and said to call him. The very gracious coach did just that. He explained to John that Alex is not prohibited from trying out, but expressed his concern about Alex's safety. The coach suggested it might be better for all of us if Alex was the manager of the team, not a player. I could not have agreed more.

Alex weighs 145 pounds, but stands at only 4 feet 10 inches. Her reflexes aren't fast enough to avoid a charging adolescent boy or a speeding football. We agreed to try to convince her that being the team manager was a better idea. After an entire summer of telling her stories about the perils of football, we successfully persuaded her to become the manager. John called the coach, and from the other room, I could hear his sigh of relief over the phone.

As parents of a child with Down syndrome, our dilemma — or perhaps responsibility — is to recognize that deep down in our hearts, we know that Alex must learn to fend for herself, promote herself and find the strength to succeed in any situation. But we also need to teach and prepare her for a world after us in which she might not always recognize real and perceived threats and dangers. Advocacy is the key to an independent or semi-independent lifestyle, and since Alex is already 17, I think about this every day.

I have always advocated and will continue to do so on behalf of Alex. But in order for her to really succeed in life, just like every other child, it's critical that she also learns to find her voice, recognize where her strengths lie and act on those skills.

From Grief to Celebration

VERB 8: Expect the Best

I believe strongly that no one should be judged by his or her cognitive abilities and those with Down syndrome are no exception. Alex is not a young woman to be underestimated, and I find myself continually reminding her teachers to raise their expectations. At the same time, I try to understand their perceptions were formed long before they ever met her.

When Alex wants something to happen in her life, it will happen, just like with my other kids. For instance, she loves music and drama, and for the last three years, just as with sports, Alex has demanded the drama teacher give her a part in the school play. I never had any doubt she'd be cast (particularly because in cases like these, she doesn't take no for an answer).

However, on other occasions, Alex may need a little more time to process and proceed. It's never a lack of understanding, merely the mechanism Alex uses to understand the big picture, and I always expect the best. Watching how Alex learns to learn has been fascinating. I think of it in terms of mountains, valleys and plateaus.

Early on I was concerned Alex was not acquiring basic skills because she was so much slower than her peers. However, through enough research, reading materials and conversations with other parents of children with special needs, I gained the understanding that her process was different, which in turn enabled me to gain confidence in Alex's future. We found a new normal and learned to embrace it.

Alex retains endless bits of information in her brain and when it all makes sense to her, she processes it and it becomes learning. Speech was our first experience with this. Her words were in her head, but her mind and tongue were not in concert. Actual development and practice just take a bit longer for her. Sometimes it's weeks and months, although sometimes it's just a second — it all depends on how she connects everything in her brain. But it's all in there, as she will recall the oddest memories at the most random times.

Alex's overall delays have become more pronounced as she has gotten older, but at least now I know to expect it. I remember the frustration of changing her diaper when she was three, but I believed at some point she would be toilet trained. It happened at age four, and, thankfully, it stuck. I remember the monotony of spoon-feeding her when she was three and a half. But at four she mastered the spoon, at four and a half the fork, and the knife at eight. Now she makes her own breakfast and lunch. If we're not home, I leave a frozen dinner that she prepares for herself. I always expected these milestones would be reached, but she has nevertheless exceeded my expectations.

When Alex was finally toilet trained, it felt to me as if she had scaled the highest mountain. Other times, like when we have challenges with speech (grammar continues to be troublesome for her), it feels as if she's fallen back into a valley. Mostly we spend a lot of time on plateaus, where I feel she might never master a new skill. But then she does — always. I expect the best, but have learned to adjust as needed. This is especially true when we're in a valley, or experiencing a temporary lack of growth.

When Alex was in a new school district in seventh grade, she seemed to be getting the same homework over and over. I finally asked the teacher why, and she told me that Alex had not mastered the lesson. The teacher's expectation was for Alex to be able to retell the story. Even Alex will tell you she is not a trained seal and will not regurgitate on command.

I asked the teacher to move on, go back to Alex a few weeks later and then ask about the previous lesson. I explained she was, indeed, learning, but needed more processing time. Through my advocating and understanding, the teacher also learned to expect the best in Alex and she will prove herself time and again. Plateaus are simply resting places for her to take time to catch up.

Climbing educational mountains is something Alex does frequently; she's always learning. But she's learned to climb mountains literally, too. It came as a pleasant surprise to me how quickly Alex learned to ski, and recognizing how much she enjoyed it, we really pushed her to master it. Because it's a sport that requires so much gear, nobody looks at her differently, and I believe it equalizes her. Participating in the Special Olympics for skiing has also further boosted her confidence and pride. The fact that Alex had male instructors was important to this huge achievement. We joke that Alex's extra chromosome interacts much better with people with Y chromosomes.

I'm always trying to figure out what makes Alex tick and what I can say or do to help facilitate the learning process in her brain. I often need to remind myself that she's different than me and different than her siblings. But at the same time, she's like us in many ways. She can step up to the plate and perform. She can read, write, multiply, subtract and play sports at a high school level. Alex has a promising future and a fulfilling life ahead of her. I'm proud of her and her determination to have a great life.

In the last 17 years, I've learned to love the mountains, dread the valleys and begrudgingly appreciate the respite of the plateaus. But always, I believe. Alex never disappoints.

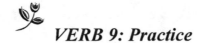

VERB 9: Practice

Healthy Skepticism

After Alex was born and while we were in our research stage, I actively sought out parents of older children with Down syndrome. I read as much as I could and made what seemed like millions of phone calls. I wanted to know exactly what Alex's life would be like, and what I needed to do to prepare for her world.

The parents I met were helpful and hopeful. The common theme was "treat her just like a normal child." This turned out to be far and away the best advice, and I never stop expecting Alex to act and behave just like her sister and brother. Sometimes she doesn't, but I never lower my expectations for her.

I also learned that any book copyrighted before 1990 was potentially suspect. In the 1980s a silent revolution occurred in Down syndrome research as well as in the quality of lives of children with special needs. By the early '90s these rebellious thoughts began to appear in print, and new and enlightened materials became available to new parents just like us.

These parents became more actively involved in their children's education, the Americans with Disabilities Act passed in 1990 and children with special needs were included in regular classrooms. The literature was updated, success stories of Down syndrome children and adults were published, and by the early '90s bookstores began to carry these words of hope and promise. Think Chris Burke in "Sesame Street" and "Life Goes On."

This revolution didn't happen by chance, and it's certainly not over, but it has changed our literature and our outlook. The revolution was further supported by the evolution of the Internet and access to the wealth of information available. Blogs, personal stories and the websites of national and local Down syndrome support groups have improved all of our abilities to learn. I am incredibly grateful for this and will always do my part to carry this message of promise to the next group of parents.

I learned very quickly that, as is the case with many mothers and their children, I know Alex best. I'm the one who always expects the best from her when others may not. To me, this almost automatically means others' expectations of Alex could be based on erroneous facts and/or experiences from years ago when early intervention programs did not exist and ignorance did. I've programmed myself to be doubtful of many of the insights shared by Alex's educators, but I endeavor to listen as best as I can. Practicing healthy skepticism and maintaining a positive and helpful attitude about Alex and her capabilities is essential to her development and education.

All children with special needs are tested to determine their IQ scores at some point. In my opinion, this is one of the dumbest indicators of anything I have ever come across. However, it's also one of those ridiculous requirements to classify a child, which in turn is needed to provide services. Alex does not perform on command; she sees no sense in random tests and usually does not cooperate. This doesn't bother me in the least, but it does produce the lowest IQ scores you can imagine. If I believed her IQ score, then I would assume she is unable to perform the basic skills needed in life.

Although Alex's IQ level indicated the following should not be true, here is a list of Alex's skills (at age 17).

She can:

Personal
- Dress herself
- Brush her teeth and hair
- Attend to all personal matters, i.e. showers and other girl stuff

Academic
- Read, write and comprehend at a third- to fifth-grade level
- Add, subtract, multiply and divide at a third- to fifth-grade level
- Memorize her class schedule
- Navigate the busy hallways at school to get to all her classes on time
- Unlock her school and gym lockers
- Bring home oral messages from her teachers
- Participate in science labs, presentations, etc.

Sports
- Ski
- Play basketball, soccer, tennis, softball
- Run, skip, hop and jump
- Bowl
- Ice skate
- Ride horses

Other life skills
- Express her needs and wants
- Clean her room/make her bed
- Do her laundry
- Prepare all her meals (in the microwave)
- Count money
- Find her way home
- Stay home by herself
- Cross the street
- Recognize "stranger danger"

As of today, Alex cannot:

Academic
- Stay focused when she does not understand a subject matter
- Comprehend reading materials beyond a fifth-grade level
- Do algebra or geometry problems

Sports
- Ride a two-wheel bicycle

Other Life skills
- Drive a car
- Take the public bus without supervision
- Monitor her food intake

I trust my daughter, my intuition and myself when I read or hear of things that children and adults with Down syndrome can't or will never be able to do. My healthy skepticism — brought to fruition through research, understanding and expecting the best — has proven this to me time and time again. I'm always skeptical when Alex says she can't do something, and I use the verb "understand" to try and figure out from where this obstinacy or lack of cooperation stems.

Self-advocating will aid Alex in proving to the world that she is not her IQ score, as well as prove my point that you should never believe what others expect. John, Courtney, Tom, Alex and I know what she can do. Alex can and will do whatever she wants. "Can't" is the worst four-letter word you can utter in our house.

From Grief to Celebration

VERB 10: Plan

In our world, "plan" has two practical applications. Alex plans for Alex, and John and I plan for Alex.

Alex is the most organized person I know. As with most people with Down syndrome, she's a visual learner. She follows instruction well, but for her to really learn and retain information it must be written down. Alex knows this and writes things down all the time. I find stickies and notes all over her room of things she must do, or things she wants to do. She gives me her Christmas list in June and her birthday list in December.

Every Sunday, I print out our weekly schedule and put it on the refrigerator. If I'm late, Alex reminds me. If I forget one of Alex's activities, she writes it on the calendar for me. She adds items to the grocery list or movies she wants to see. Her school planner is similar — not only does she have her homework assignments, but she also has her social activities.

Alex uses her cell phone as an alarm as well as a calendar. Her phone goes off at 6:45 every morning. (Although getting her out of bed is a different story. Just like my other kids — and me! — she doesn't like to wake up.) I often hear the calendar go off on her phone, letting her know her favorite TV show is on, but often it's also a reminder to do her homework.

Before the birth of each of our children, John and I planned and dreamed of their futures. Schools, sports and other extracurricular activities are all a part of what forms our children's futures, and we have adjusted, managed and guided as needed when new or stronger interests emerge.

Our hopes and dreams for Alex's future are the same as for Courtney and Tom's. I want all three of my kids to have fulfilling jobs, healthy relationships and lives overflowing with love. I want them to give back to their communities and be grateful for the opportunities they have in their lives. However, in Alex's case we've needed to be more diligent in working towards a different type of future, which is simultaneously one of independence and safety.

When Alex was born we grieved for the future we imagined she would never have. I know this is the reaction many parents have when a child with special needs is born. We perceived it to be gloomy because she has Down syndrome. I now know, through research, Alex's future will be different than her siblings', but that's not necessarily a bad thing.

It's unlikely Alex will have children of her own. Men with Down syndrome are generally unable to have children, and women have a 50 percent chance of having a child with Down syndrome. Alex will probably not give me a grandchild and if that's what's best for her, then that's all that matters. Alex's future is about her, not me.

Our current planning assignment, and one that will last for the next five years, is to determine a safe place for Alex to live. John and I love to talk about the days when we become empty nesters. We love our kids, but I know we can love them just as much when they live somewhere else. Courtney is already in college and Tom will be leaving in two and a half years. Empty nest syndrome is around the corner, and we are really looking forward to our future!

As parents of a child with special needs, we do need to work a bit harder than most of our friends to make our dream a reality. College is a possibility, as is the legally mandated Transition Program that allows Alex to stay in the public school system until she turns 21.

It's Alex's dream and ours for her to eventually live independently with a minimal amount of supervision. I've researched a number of assisted living facilities for adults with disabilities but have yet to find one that will be a good fit for Alex. I also do not believe in that option for Alex.

We're even considering starting our own community for her called WindWalkers Ranch, which is an extension of an equine assisted therapeutic riding program that Alex currently participates in. We're working to make it a residential community for adults with and without disabilities in a ranch setting built around horses, community and love.

Alex will also need to find a meaningful job to pay her rent and bills. She doesn't want to be a vice president at a large bank, or a real estate developer. Those were our dream, not hers. We're hopeful she'll enjoy a career that requires skills like being organized and detailed (or telling people what to do, because we already know that's something in which she excels). On our ranch, she could manage the lesson schedule and participate in ranch duties.

We dream of an independent and safe life for Alex. She needs a comfortable and nurturing environment in which genuinely caring people surround her and help her succeed in her career and relationships. As with Courtney and Tom, it's essential to John and me that Alex lead a fulfilling life. And with the reality of all dreams, to make them come true we must plan, plan and plan some more.

BONUS VERB: Celebrate

Everyday we celebrate the pure joy of Alex, our beautiful daughter, sister, granddaughter, niece, cousin, student and friend who continues to enrich our lives in unimaginable and immeasurable ways. Her very existence has given us the power to become better people and more empathetic community members.

We have met tremendous children with special needs and their families, as well as scores of remarkable adults with special needs. We have had the good fortune to work with caring and skilled professionals because of Alex. We celebrate her life as a gift and privilege to so many people in so many ways.

Alex teaches us not to sweat the small stuff, to take our lives one day at a time, all the while enjoying the present and the passage of time. Of course there are challenges in Alex's life as well as ours, but we do our best to pick the moment each day that is worthy of a celebration instead of cursing the darker ones. We never have to look too far to find a lesson learned through or from Alex. And in that, we delight.

Families of special kids learn early on that their children don't rush through life. Alex is no exception, her lack of urgency in everything has been apparent her whole life. She takes longer to get ready in the morning, longer with her meals, and her showers last forever. She enjoys picking out her clothes, savoring her food and the feeling of warm water on her body. She follows a simple philosophy: Why rush?

We make adjustments for Alex and give her extra time, but sometimes it's still not enough. It doesn't matter how long we give her because she always chugs along at her own speed. We call this "Stop and Smell the Roses" Syndrome.

While we have frustrating moments trying to get Alex to move along at our speed, we've also learned to celebrate the journey of life along the way. She has literally reminded us that roses are worth stopping for; we admire their beauty and smell their sweet perfume. Her speed can either elevate or alleviate our stress levels; it's up to us which way it'll go at any given moment. No one wants to be late, but how worth it is it to get stressed out over a delayed minute here and there? Sometimes it's fun to admire a cute baby passing by in a stroller for an extra moment, or spend a few more minutes giggling at the comics in the paper. We celebrate that reminder.

Alex is also the one who wants family game night. She cherishes whatever moments we can all spend together, and supports us in our individual pursuits as much as we do in hers. She's in the front row at each of her sister's plays, bundled up on the slopes for all of her brother's snowboard competitions, her face beaming with pride each and every time. She begs John for special father-daughter time, and relishes being with him, no matter the activity. And even though I can't imagine anything more tedious, she even comes to every one of my tennis matches, celebrating my winning points as well as those of my opponents.

Alex doesn't rush through life, nor does she waste a moment. She's the most magical, loyal and truest person I know. Alex's hugs or the bestowal of her beautiful smile brighten my days and my heart. She is the sunshine in our lives — mine, John's, Courtney's and Tom's.

In many ways, I feel like the guardian of this extraordinary individual, the steward of her life, the protector of her magic. Every day I thank the universe for giving us Alex. I don't know why we've been so lucky, but I do know she has taught me an extraordinary lesson that I am obligated to celebrate and share.

I see skies of blue and clouds of white
The bright blessed day, the dark sacred night
And I think to myself what a wonderful world

Perhaps I'm a Pollyanna, and if so, I am grateful. I strive every day to make the world a better place for my family and all children with special needs. The process to get where I am today might have been through baby steps, and my ability to bring our lessons to others through even tinier steps, but I believe I have and can continue to make a difference to so many others through telling Alex's story.

In the end, Alex has helped us recognize we need to listen to her and the universe she has opened up wide to all of us. And in case we forget, she always has the final word — literally. Every night, we share the same exchange:

Alex: "I love you."

Me: "I love you more."

Alex: "I love you best."

Me: "I love you bestest."

Alex: "I love you est."

Me: "I love you er."

Alex: "Mom, that is not a word."

There really is a lesson of celebration in this for everyone of us.

Giving Back

Early intervention revolutionized the way children with Down syndrome were educated, research in Down syndrome is revolutionizing the way our children will live and age. I support this initiative and will be donating a percentage of sales of this book to Research Down Syndrome. For more information go to their website www.researchds.org

There are many organizations that have helped us in the days and years since Alex's birth. These organizations are run by passionate and caring professionals and in many cases parents. A percentage of sales of this book will also be donated to the following:

National Association for Down Syndrome, where Sheila taught us Alex was a baby first.
www.NADS.org

The Roaring Fork Mountain Nino's, Alex's Special Olympics Team, where Cammi and Paul treat all the athletes as athletes first.
www.roaringforkmountainninos.org

And the organization that is near and dear to my heart:

WindWalkers Equine Assisted Learning and Therapy Center to support WindWalkers Ranch. Not only is Molly a dedicated and passionate Executive Director, she teaches us every day to believe.
www.windwalkerstrc.org

Acknowledgements

This work is based on my experience as the mother of an extraordinary girl. I don't pretend to know all the answers, and can only use my own experiences to try to help others understand, accept and rejoice in the journey we have undertaken.

A huge thanks to everyone who helped me realize this dream to share my story. There are more than I can acknowledge in these few short sentences.

First, to all the people I have met in the blog community. These families from across the world are always there to share stories, provide encouragement and wipe away the tears. I'd especially like to thank Justin, the dad of a young son with Down syndrome, who created an extraordinary website called Down Syndrome.com which can be found at www.downsyndrome.com. This vehicle has given people from the around the world the opportunity to communicate and share.

I'd like to acknowledge two of my new cyber friends, Tiffany at www.superdownsy.blogspot.com and Lisa at www.starrlife.wordpress.com. These women are loving and caring moms with excellent blogs. They are examples of so many other moms, dads, families and professionals who are making a difference in the lives of our children and everyone they meet in their journeys.

Thanks to my talented editor, Meredith Carroll, at www.meredithcarroll.com, my creative graphic designer, Erin, at www.rainydaydesigns.org, and my very supportive friend, Michele, at www.michelecozzens.com. Michele is a very gifted author and tried so hard to teach me "show don't tell." You can judge my ability to learn.

Please read all about Alex and her life on our blog: *The Ordinary Life of an Extraordinary Girl*, we can be found at www.downsyndrometeenager.blogspot.com.

You will also find a link to buy more copies of this book at our blog, I am happy to provide wholesale pricing for any orders over 25.

If you would like to contact me, I'd love to hear from you via email at theextraordinarygirlllc@gmail.com

December 2010

About the Author

My name is Gary, which is short for Margaret. My father named me, and often people ask me if my father wanted a boy. My father says that was not the case; he wanted to name me after my mother Margaret. He claims the *gare* in the middle inspired him to create the nickname Gary. It has been with me from birth, and is something that makes me different.

I was born in New Jersey and attended college in New York. I worked on Wall Street after college, and was transferred to San Francisco when I was 26. It was there that I met my incredible husband of 22 years, John. We moved to Illinois to be near family when we were pregnant with our first child.

We lived in Illinois for 14 years and loved raising our three babies in the Midwest. It's a great family-centric part of the country, where hospitals and schools are good. We still have lots of family and very good friends there.

When our oldest was entering high school we decided it was time to realize our fantasy to live in the mountains. We had always envisioned a different high school experience for our children, and when the opportunity presented itself, we moved. After a period of adjustment, our kids have embraced the mountain lifestyle and almost thanked us for uprooting them from all of their friends.

We live outside a small but renown resort town and enjoy all the benefits of being "locals." We ski and snowshoe in the winter, and in the summer we raft, hike, swim, bike and play lots of tennis.

Our school district is rural, our hospital 30 minutes away and the only chain store, Walmart, is a 25-mile drive. Life in the mountains is very different than the suburbs of Chicago, but I wouldn't change anything about our journey.

I have been a trader, a banker, a learning manager and a facilitator. I enjoyed all of these careers and learned something from every one of them. I traveled around the country and parts of the world while working in banking, and had the opportunity to meet hundreds of people from incredible cultures that are so different than mine. Now it is time to put all these skills together and embrace a new career where perhaps I can make a difference – writing.

This first book was borne from a year and half of blogging experience. I hope to reach others, especially those with younger children with Down syndrome, and help them learn that the future is bright.

Maybe the writing skills I learned in college as a history major are finally coming in handy.